STRINGSTASTIC
Level 1
CELLO

By Lorraine Chai

USA Edition

STRINGSTASTIC

PO BOX 815 Epping NSW 1710 Australia
www.stringstastic.com
Copyright © 2019 Lorraine Chai
First Published 2019
2nd Edition 2020
USA Edition 2021

Book design by Meilisa Lengkong

All rights reserved.
Reproduction in whole or in part for any use whatsoever is strictly prohibited.

THE AUTHOR
LORRAINE CHAI

Lorraine is a multitalented instrumentalist and an international educator. She graduated from the Sydney Conservatorium of Music with a Bachelor of Music Studies in 2008 and completed her Graduate Diploma of Education at the Australian Catholic University a year later.

Having grown up with a musical family, Lorraine began piano lessons at the age of four and violin at the age of six, giving her first violin performance at just seven years of age. Lorraine started teaching violin at the age of 14 and founded a string ensemble at her local church. From there, teaching and performing became her passion.

Lorraine loves finding new and exciting ways students can learn their instrument in a classroom setting as well as in private lessons. Along her musical journey and exposure to the various educational methods including Kodaly, Suzuki, Orff, and Dalcroze, Lorraine has also attended Alexander Technique workshops, and has found that she can integrate these various methods into her own teaching technique for the benefit of her students.

Lorraine has extensive ensemble and orchestral experience in Malaysia and in Australia. Lorraine currently the Music Director of Stringstastic Pty Ltd and is an active member with the Australian Strings Association, AUSTA NSW.
She also co-ordinates instrumental programmes and runs string ensembles for some of Sydney's most celebrated schools.

PREFACE

This Stringstastic cello book series is specifically designed for beginner cellist aged 6-12 years. Stringstastic Level 1 for cello players introduces young players to the world of cello playing and music theory through games and fun graphics to assist the young cellists better understand the instrument and to learn music theory in an enjoyable way.
This Stringstastic series can be used in a private lesson or along side the violin and viola book series in a classroom setting.

For extra resources, go to www.stringstastic.com to download them for free.

Have fun!!

ACKNOWLEDGEMENT

This book was made possible with the encouragement of my family and loved ones. I would like to thank the following for their advice and input in making this book possible.

Dr. Rita Crews OAM, FMusA (honoris causa), PhD(UNE), BA(Hons), AMusTCL, GradCertDistEd (UNE), FMusicolASMC, HonFNMSM, DipMus (honoris causa) (AICM) MIMT, MACE, MMTA, JP.

Dr. Anthony Clarke DMA, MMus, Grad Dip, BMus Ed, DSCM, FTCL, LMusA, AMusA

Helen Tuckey PG Dip Music (Manhattan School of Music), AMusA, MIMT, DipArts(music) (Victorian College of the Arts)

David Pereira DSCM, MMus (Indiana University)

Ismail Farid LTCL, a prominent orchestral director, music educator and performer

CONTENTS

4	STRING FAMILY
5	THE CELLO PARTS
7	SIMON SAYS
8	TWO WAYS OF
9	MUSIC STAFF
11	BASS CLEF
13	CELLO STRINGS
14	BAR LINES
15	READING NOTES
20	POSITION OF STEMS
23	NOTE VALUES
27	WHAT HAVE WE LEARNED SO FAR?
29	RESTS
31	TIME SIGNATURE
33	REVISION
35	ACCIDENTALS
38	D STRING
40	STRINGS AND NOTE NAMES
41	A STRING
43	REVISION D AND A STRING
45	G STRING
47	C STRING
49	REVISION (ON ALL STRINGS)
51	TEST

STRINGSTASTIC

String Family

Violin   Viola   Cello   Double Bass

Which is the smallest string instrument?

Which is the biggest string instrument?

Which instrument do you play?

Suzie and Tommy play in a string quartet. Suzie plays the smallest instrument while Tommy sits down playing his instrument.
Which instruments do Suzie and Tommy play?

Suzie:

Tommy:

Color in Suzie and Tommy....

The Cello Parts

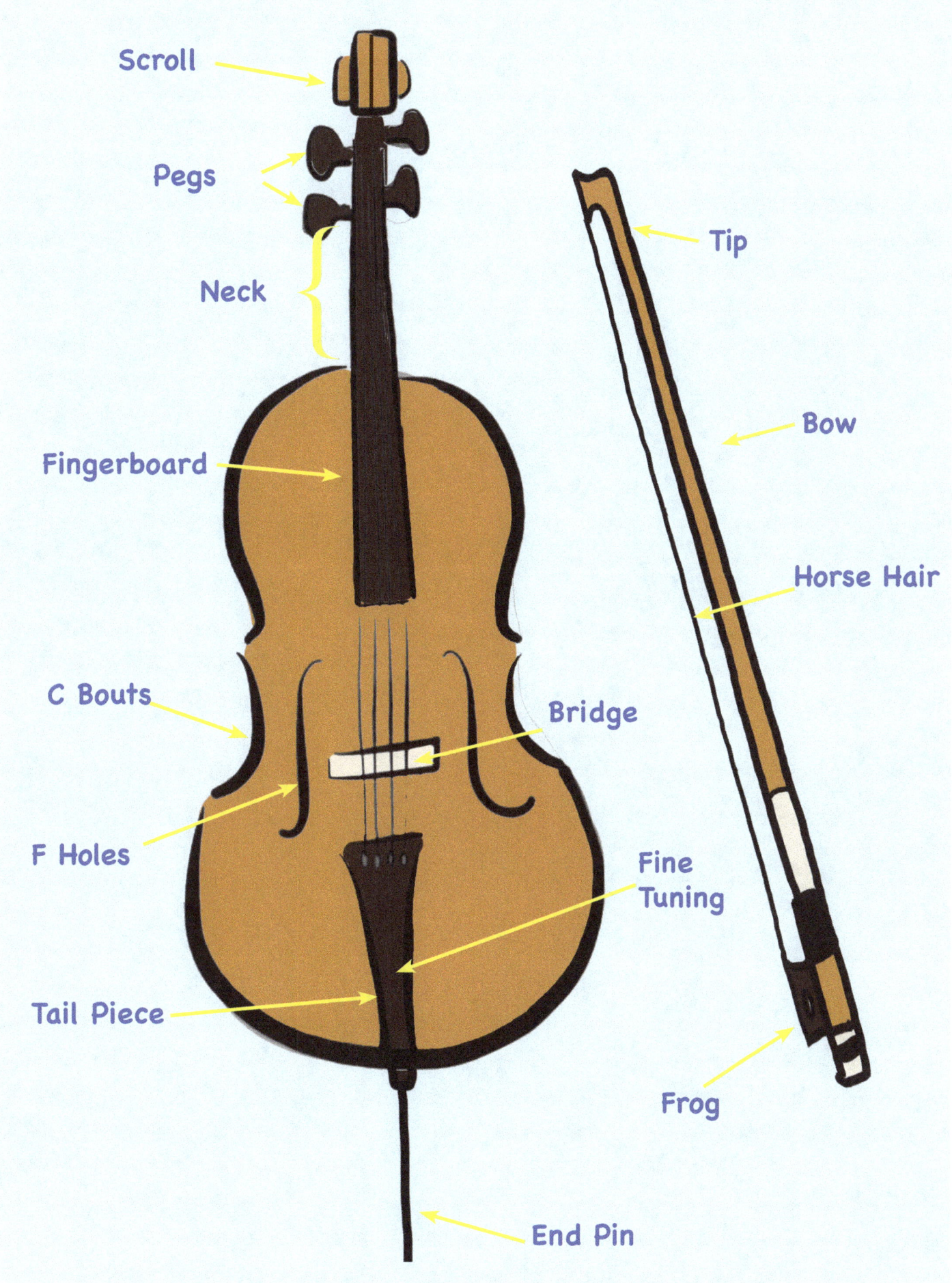

Draw the cello and bow and label their parts.

Simon Says

Your teacher will give you the instructions. You are only allowed to move 5 times in this game. See how many movements you have made by the end of it.

Sitting

1. Sit on the front half of the chair
- with your body weight on your sitting bones (your bottom). (DON'T SLOUCH OR TWIST AROUND)
2. Have your thighs slope gently down towards your knees.
3. Place your feet flat on the floor underneath your knees - this helps stabilize your body and keeps you balanced.
4. Keep shoulders down and arms loosely hanging by your sides and then gently placing your arms on your laps.

Cello Placement

1. Spread your knees apart and place the lower body of the cello between them.
(DON'T SQUEEZE THE CELLO)
2. Have the pegs by your left ear
- NOT touching them.
3. While facing forward, place the end-pin just right of your centre line.
4. Make sure your head is still free to move without hitting the peg.
5. Rest the upper body of the cello on the left side of your chest.

Now let us see if you can teach mom or dad how to hold up the cello. How did they do?

Two Ways of...

...playing the cello

	MEANING	
arco	Pulling/pushing the bow across the string	
pizzicato or pizz	Plucking the string	

Music Staff

Music is written on these lines and spaces below.

 ← This is called a staff

Trace each line with the different colors and number each line from the bottom up.

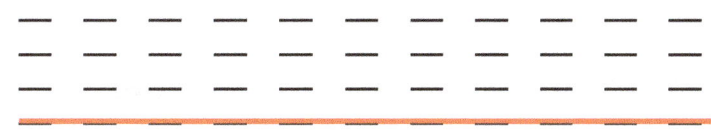

1. Red   2. Yellow   3. Blue   4. Green   5. Brown

How many lines does a staff have? _____

Draw a note through each line.

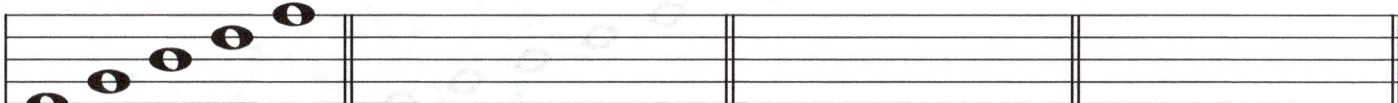

Color each space with different colors and number each space from the bottom up.

How many spaces does a staff have? _____

Draw a note in every space.

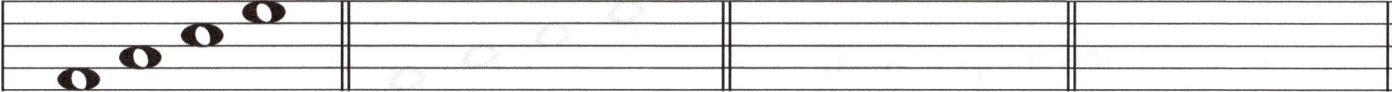

In the staff below, write an **L** below each note through a line and an **S** below each note in the spaces.

Help Suzie the Koala find her collection of shells.
Color the shells accordingly.

Shells through the lines red   Shells in the space green

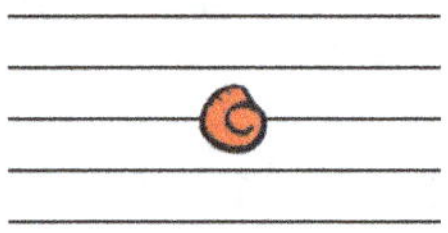

How many shells can you find?

Bass Clef

Music written for the cello uses the Bass Clef.

A bass clef looks like half of a heart shape. It is used to read low notes. Instruments such as the piano, tuba, trombone, and the double bass read from this clef.

Let us practise drawing the bass clefs below around the example before we practise drawing them on the staff.

12

Now let us trace these bass clefs on the staff and then draw 2 more of your own.

(Start on the 4th line where the red dot is.)

(The 2 little dots next to the clef goes on the top two spaces 'guarding' the point where we started drawing the clef.)

Cello Strings

Let's try and remember the names of the open strings.

(Open strings = Name of each string without placing any fingers on it.)

  C  G  D  A

Cute　　　　Girl　　　　Dances　　　　Around

This sentence is called an acronym and helps you remember the names.

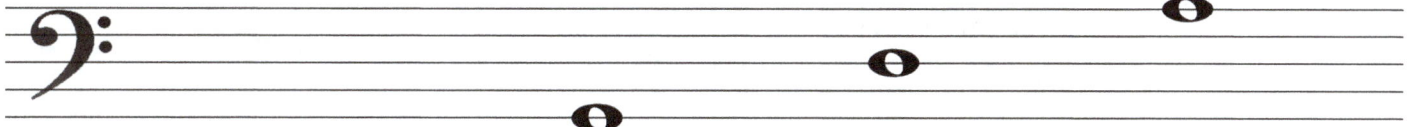

(the extra lines above and below the stave are called ledger/leger lines)

Make up your own acronym.

C_____　G_____　D_____　A_____

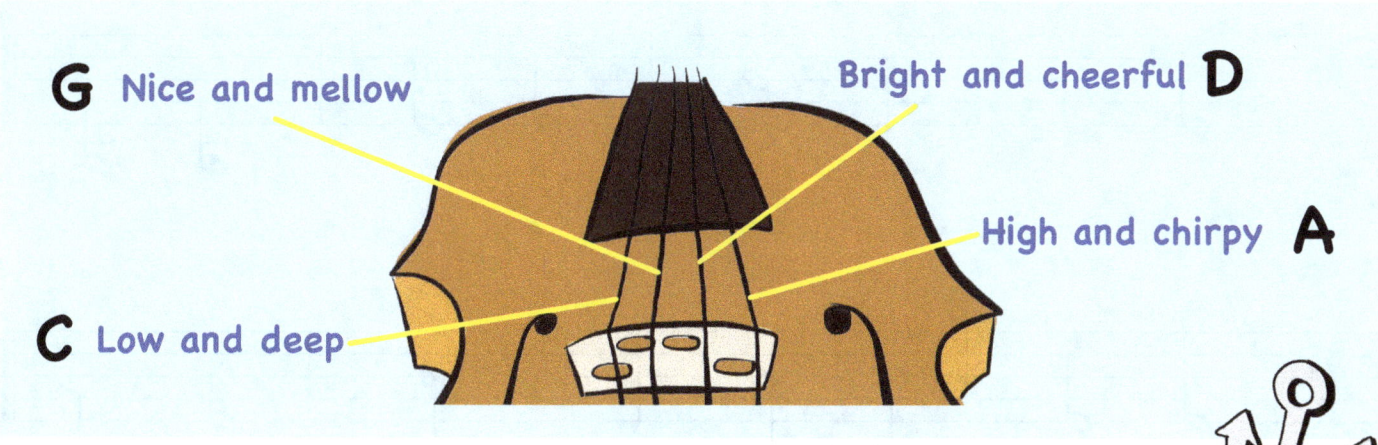

G Nice and mellow　　Bright and cheerful D

C Low and deep　　High and chirpy A

Which string produces the lowest/HEAVIEST sound? _____

Which string produces the highest/lightest sound? _____

Bar Lines

Measures are like classrooms. Each room has a certain amount of students.
Bar lines are like walls of the classrooms. And the double bar line is the end of the building.

Put an arrow where each song would end.

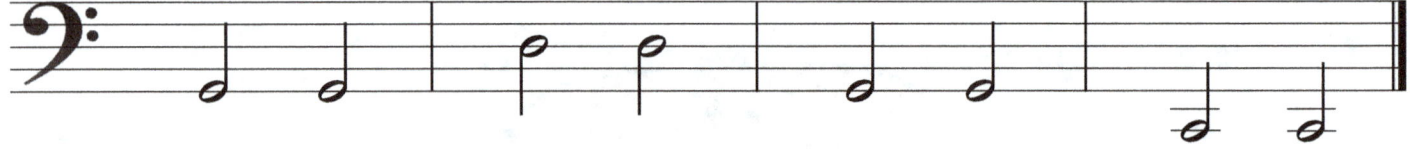

Now try and play each of these short tunes using the bow.

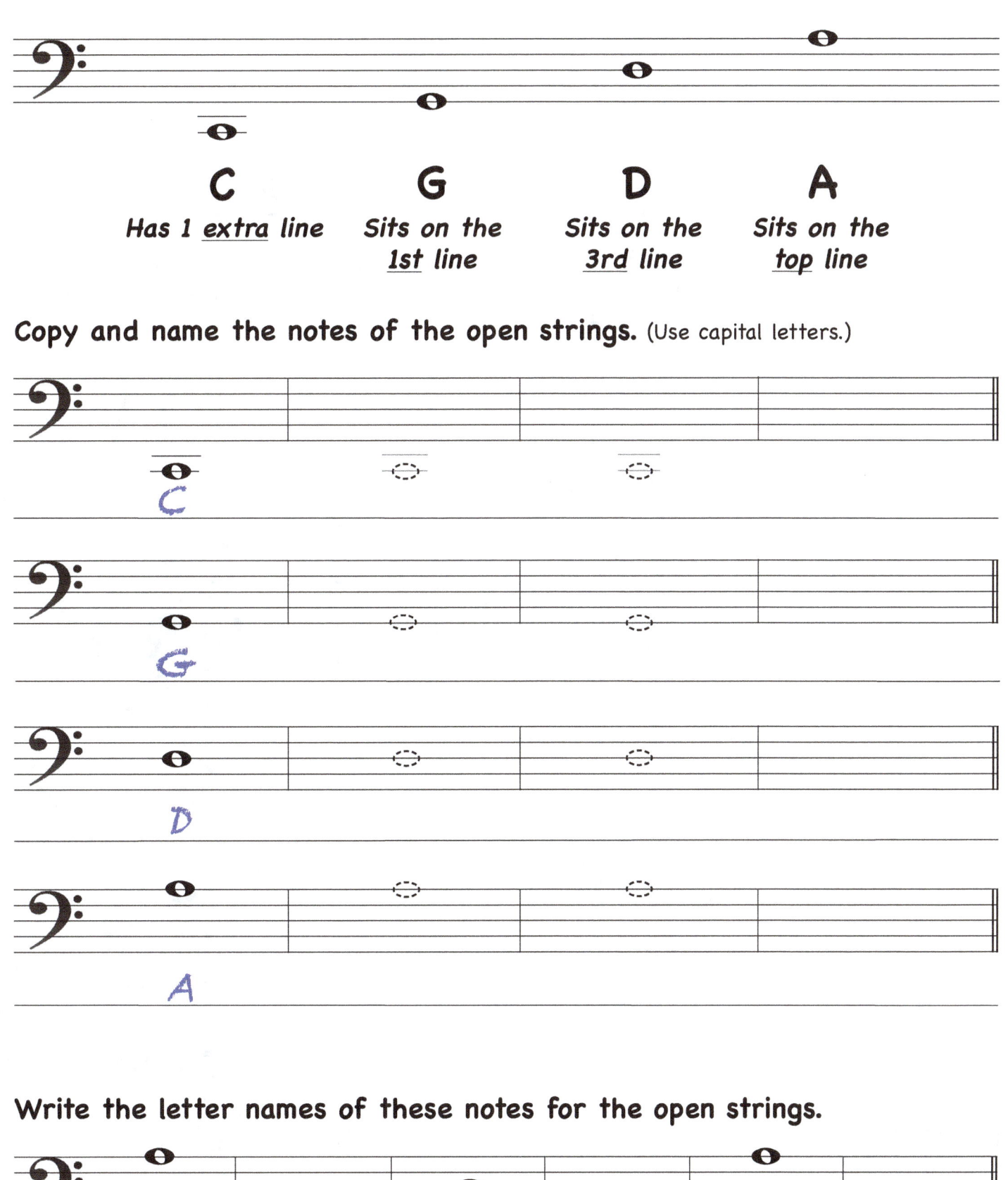

16

Draw the notes of the open strings.

A   C   G   D   A   D

Match the notes and color the correct open string.

There are other ways of remembering the names of your notes in between the open string notes.

How many lines does a staff have?

How many spaces does a staff have?

Below is how we would remember our notes using acronyms.

Gummy   Bears   Dance   Funny   Always

As for the notes in the spaces, all we need to do is use the alphabet which we already know and count up and down between the lines.
Let us see if you can figure out the notes in between.

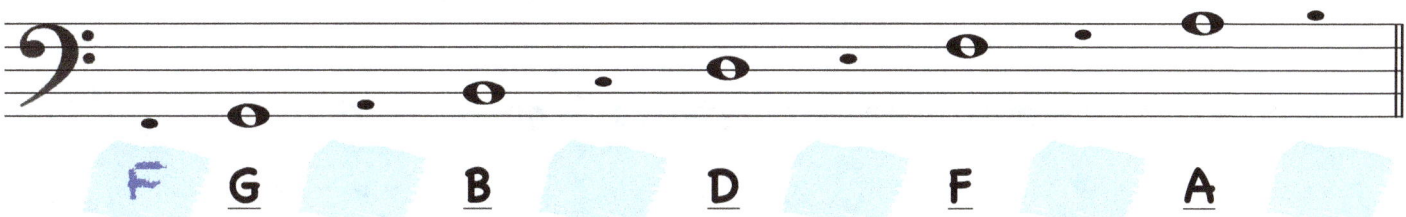

F   G   B   D   F   A

Practice saying the acronyms and see if you would be able to identify the name of the notes.

Do you remember the names of the open strings?

Name these notes.

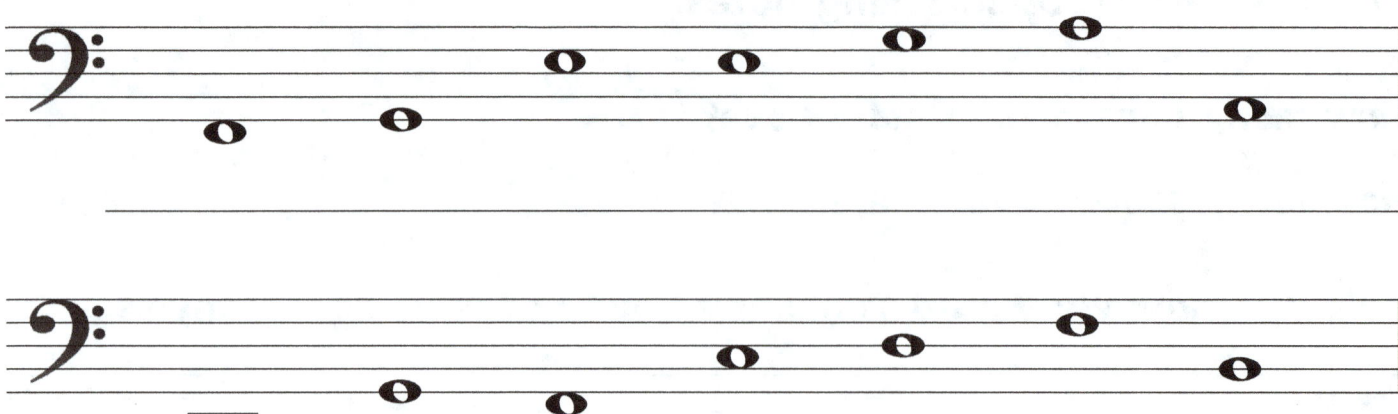

Write your alphabet from A to Z.

___

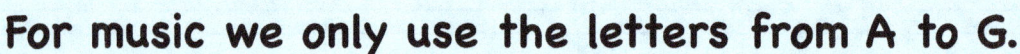

For music we only use the letters from A to G.

A   B   C   D   E   F   G

The note after G goes back to A.

See if you can memorize your alphabet backwards from G to A.

By now you should have 3 or 4 strips on your fingerboard.

Finger 1
Finger 2
Finger 3
Finger 4

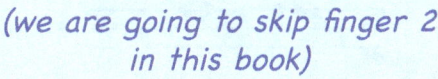

C G D A

(we are going to skip finger 2 in this book)

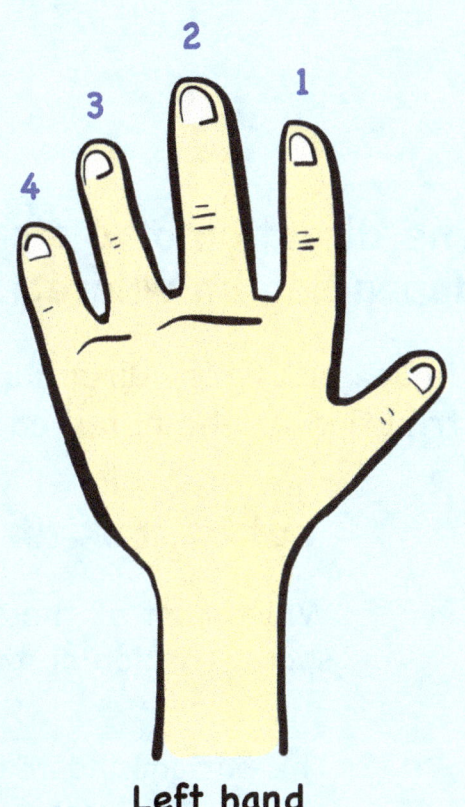

Left hand

Play each string using all fingers starting with the open string.

Call out each finger number while playing each note starting from open string (zero).

Printable flashcards and more work sheet on notes for individual open strings available at **www.stringstastic.com**

Position of Stems

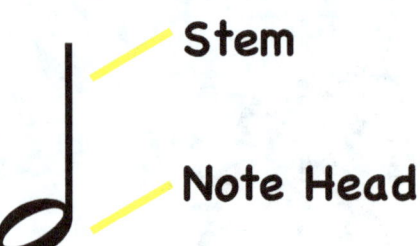

The direction of a stem can be either facing up or down depending on where the note head sits on the staff.

To figure out which direction the stem would face, think of the space distribution of the note heads and stems making them even on the staff.

Let us look at the notes on the middle line.

Which part of the staff has more space. The top or the bottom?

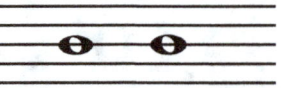

The bottom and the top part of the staff has the same amount of space.

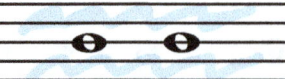

Because of this, the stems can face either upwards or downwards.

Let us look at the notes from the middle line downwards.
(Low notes)

Which part of the staff has more space. The top or the bottom?

The top part of the staff has more space.

Because of this, the stems will face upwards.
Remember that the stems are drawn on the right side of the note to make the note look like the letter 'd'.

Let us look at the notes from the middle line upwards.
(High notes)

Which part of the staff has more space. The top or the bottom?

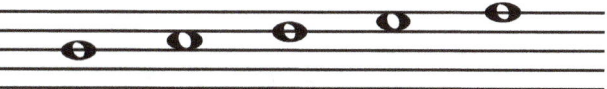

The bottom part of the staff has more space.

Because of this, the stems will face downwards.
Remember that the stems are drawn on the left side of the note to make the note look like a letter 'p'.

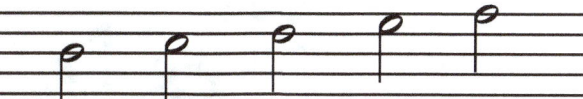

Add a stem to every note. (Think of the word **Pod**.)

Now let us name the notes above.

Some stems are facing the wrong direction. Correct them so they sit properly on the staff.

Note Values

NOTE	NOTE VALUE	NAME
♩	1	Quarter Note
♪ (half)	2	Half Note
♪. (dotted half)	3	Dotted Half Note
o	4	Whole Note

Draw the notes and their value.

Quarter Note

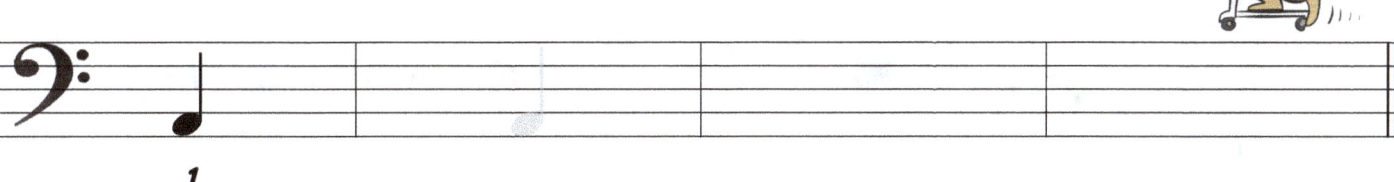

1

Half Note

2

Dotted Half Note

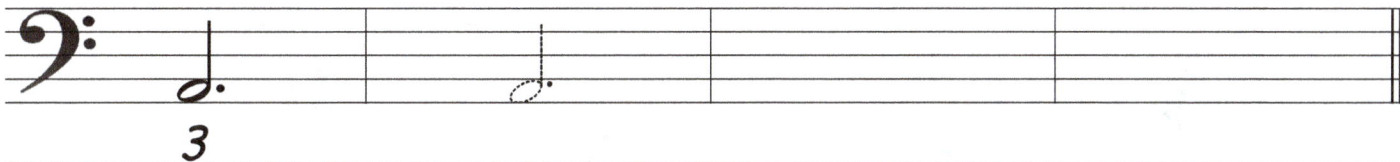

3

Whole Note

4

24

Write the note value of each note.

♩ 　 𝅝 　 𝅗𝅥. 　 𝅝 　 𝅗𝅥 　 ♩ 　 𝅗𝅥. 　 ♩

1

𝅝 　 𝅗𝅥 　 𝅗𝅥. 　 𝅗𝅥 　 ♩ 　 𝅗𝅥 　 𝅝 　 𝅗𝅥

Match the notes to the correct name.

NOTES		NAMES
𝅝 •		• Half Note
𝅗𝅥. •		• Whole Note
𝅗𝅥 •		• Dotted Half Note
♩ •		• Quarter Note

Count the number in each group. Draw the total value of each group. (Use quarter note values.)

(You can draw more than one note if the value is more than 4 counts.)

Clap and count the beats.

Using the rhythms above, write your own music using the open string notes (C, G, D, A). You can write TWO different tunes on the same rhythm.

Example:

Rhythm 1

Rhythm 2

Rhythm 3

Rhythm 4

Now try and play each of your short tunes pizz.

What have we learned so far?

1. How many strings does a cello have? Name them.

_____

2. Label and name the different parts of the cello using the words given.

bridge
end pin
bow
f holes
fine tuning
fingerboard
frog
horse hair
pegs
scroll
tail piece

3. Fill in the blanks.

SYMBOL	NAME
𝄢	
	staff
(staff lines)	
♩ (with bow mark)	

SYMBOL	NAME	COUNT
	whole note	
♩		
𝅗𝅥		
		3

4. Mark the correct string on the cello.

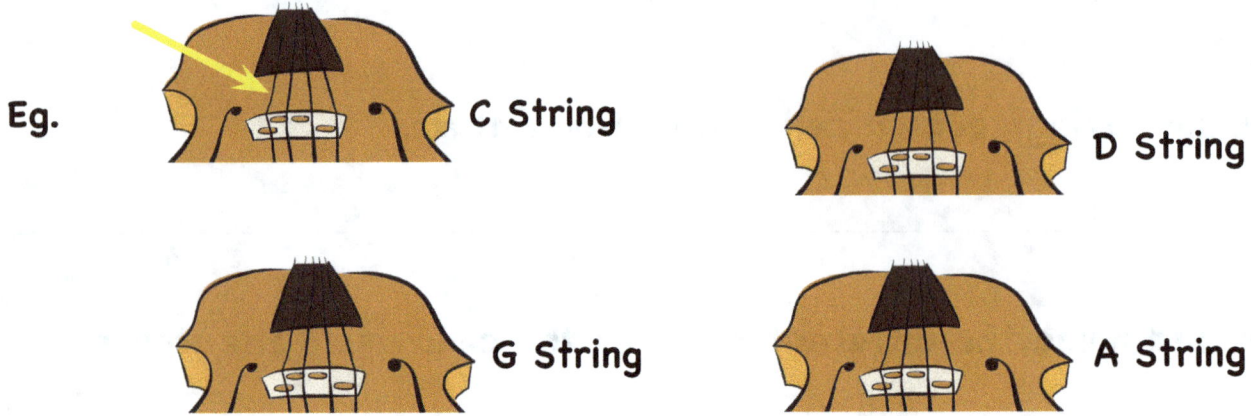

5. Draw and name these notes on the open string using whole notes.

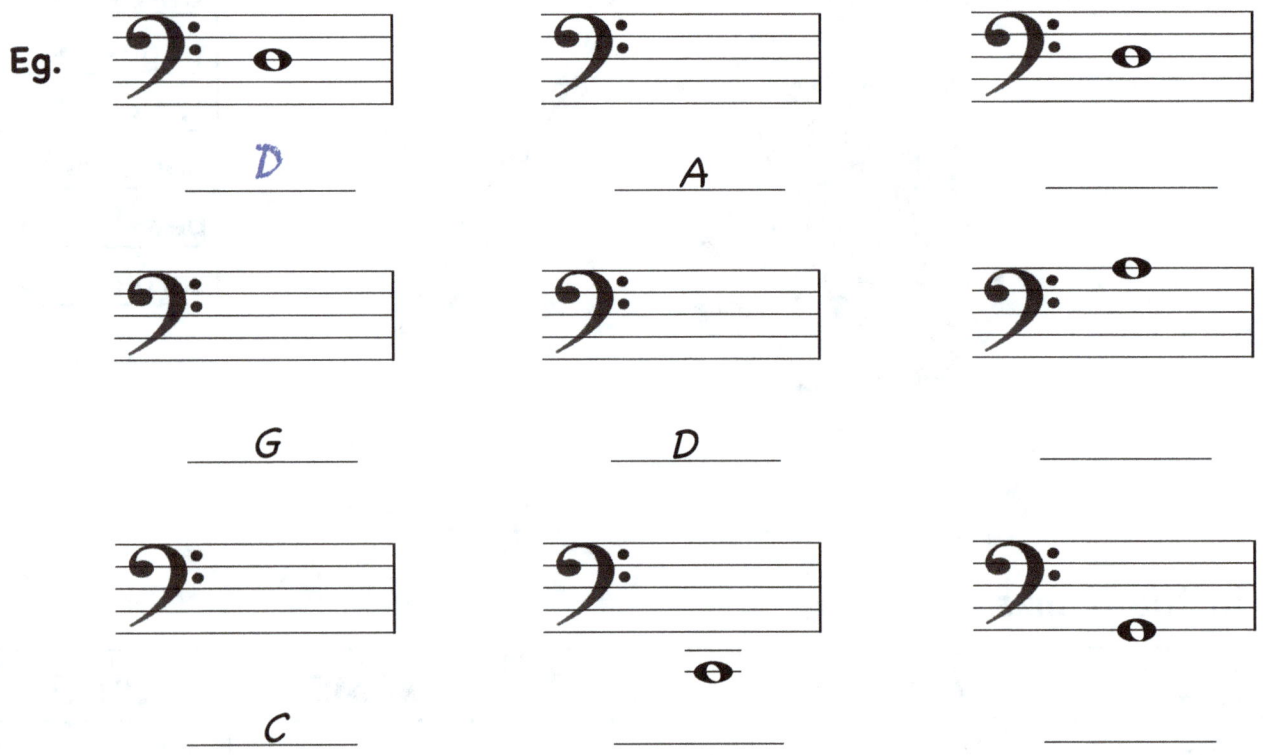

6. What letter note comes after G in music?

Rests

NOTE	REST			NOTE VALUE
♩	𝄽	If you straighten this wavy line, it looks like the number 1		1
𝅗𝅥	▬	Hat closed half full		2
𝅝	▭	You can fill more things with the hat open		4

▬ may also be used as a whole measure rest

Copy each rest and count them.

Quarter rest (lightning/slanted  + capital C)

𝄽   𝄽
1   1

Half rest (sitting on 3rd line)

▬   ▬
1 2   1 2

Whole rest (hanging on 4th line)

▭   ▭
1 2 3 4   1 2 3 4

30
Write down the value of each rest.

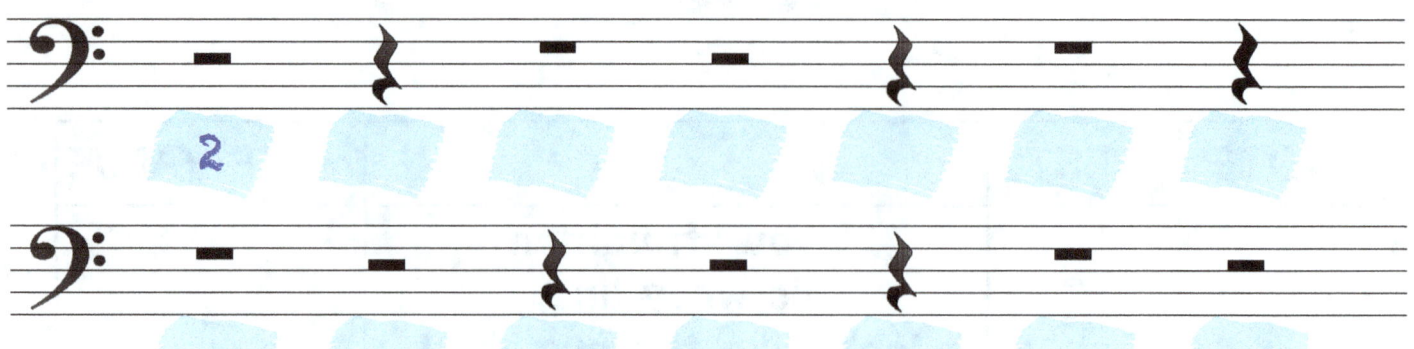

2

The sea creatures in Atlantic City live in their own luxurious underwater apartment. Help them find their correct place.

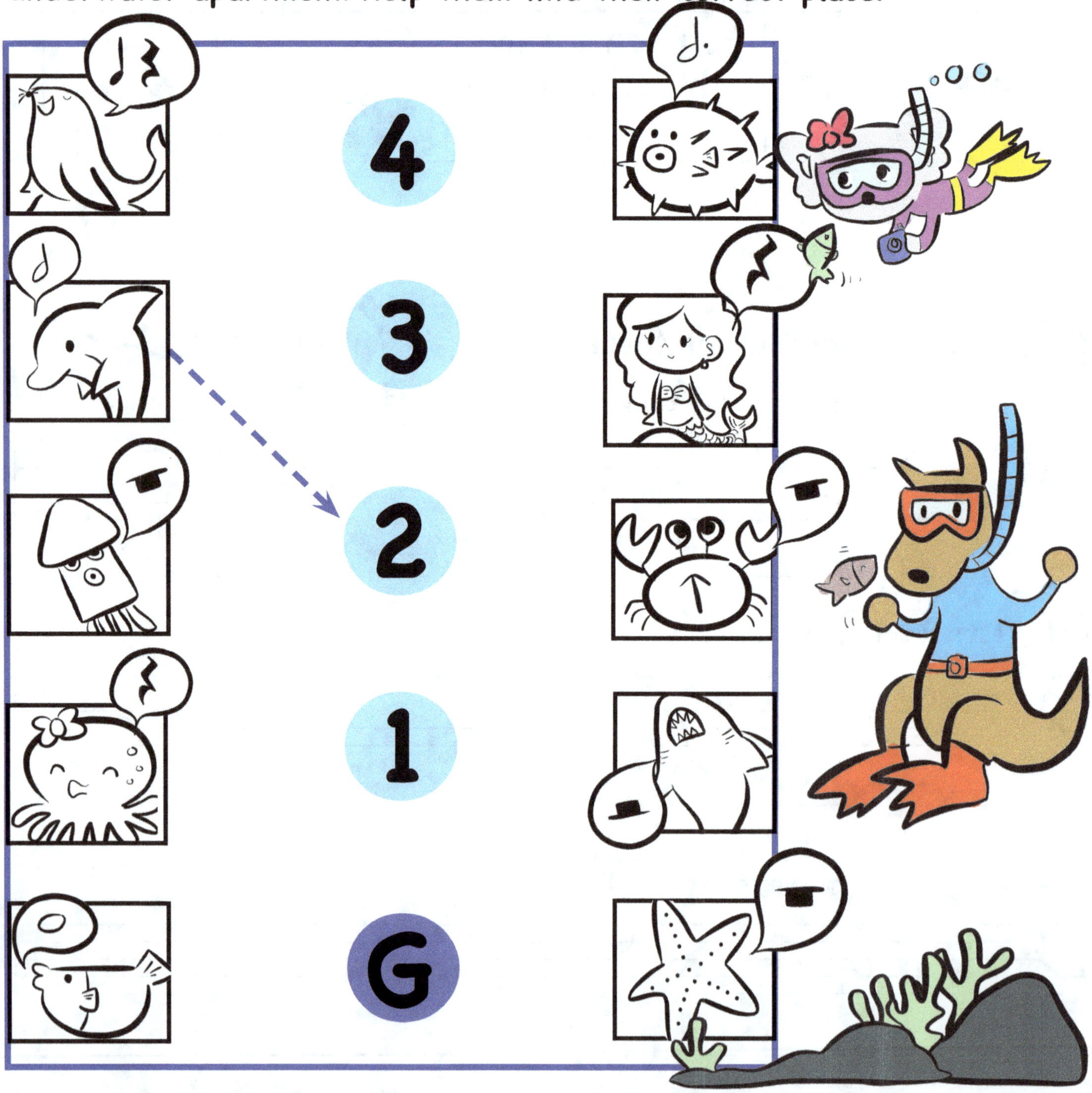

Time Signature

2/4	♩ ♩	2 quarter beats in a bar
3/4	♩ ♩ ♩	3 quarter beats in a bar
4/4	♩ ♩ ♩ ♩	4 quarter beats in a bar

Information: 3/4 top number means the number of beats in a measure.

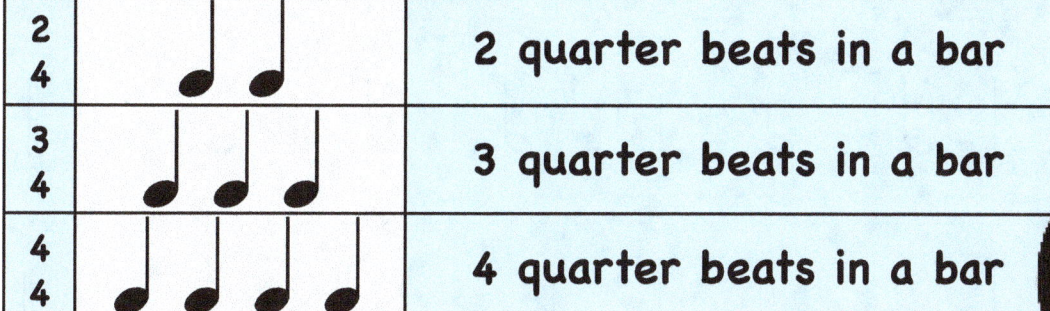

Write in the beats of each measure.

Write in the correct beats and time signature.

Put in the bar lines and write in the beats.

Revision

Complete the measures with the correct rests.

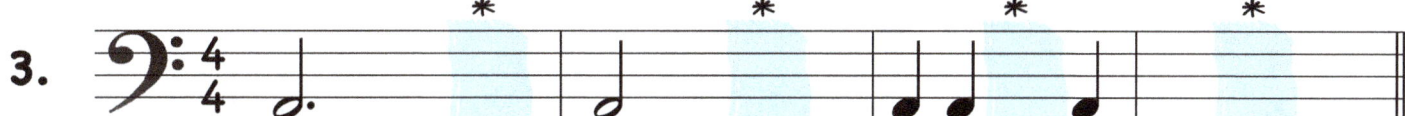

Tip: Rests are normally drawn starting on the 3rd space of the staff

Complete each measure with one of these notes.

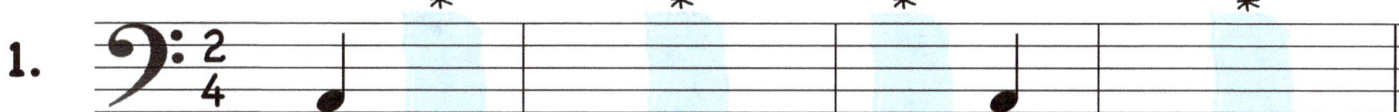

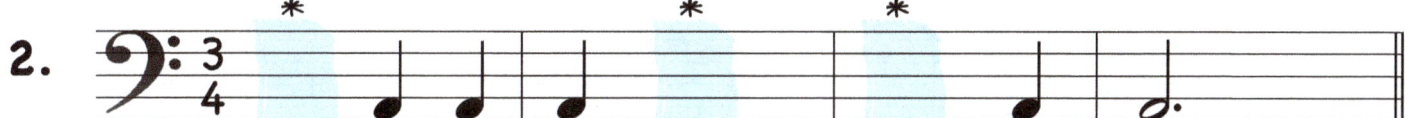

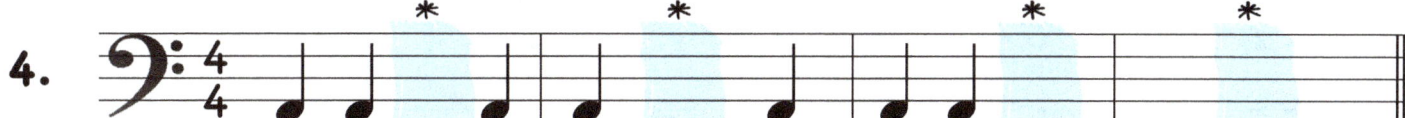

34

Write in the beats for each of these measures.

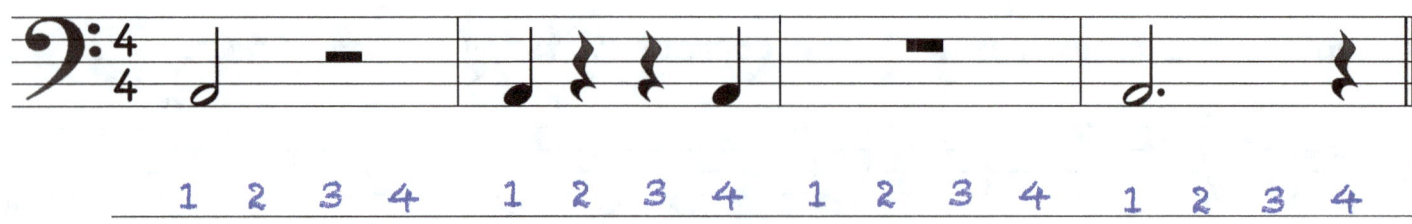

1 2 3 4   1 2 3 4   1 2 3 4   1 2 3 4

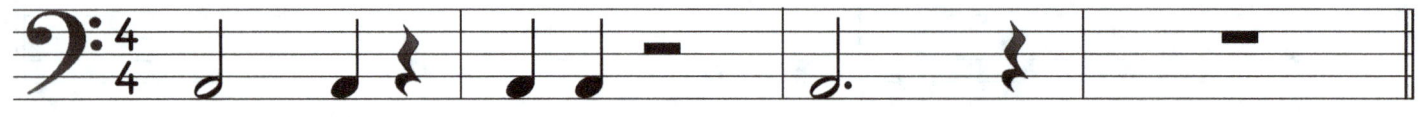

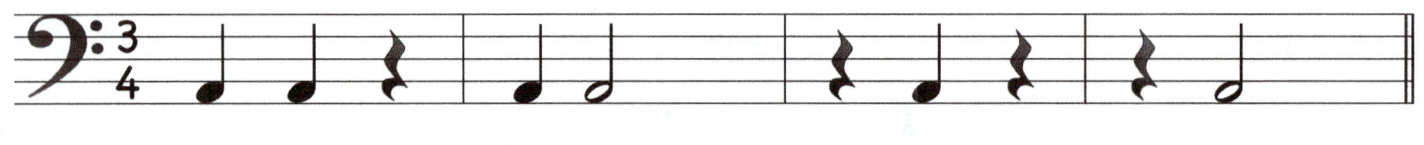

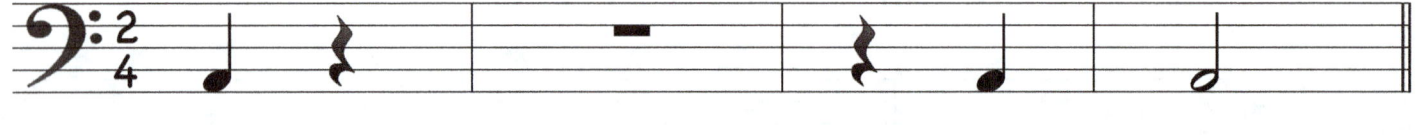

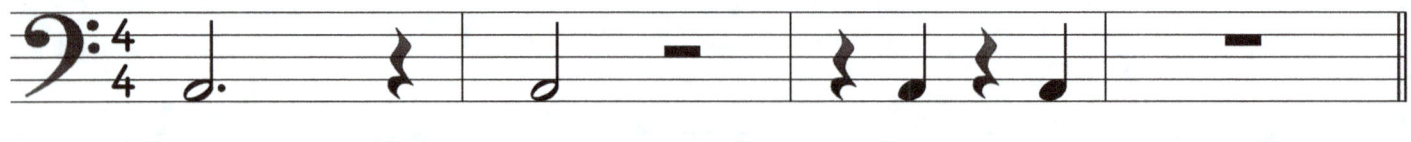

Accidentals

♭ Flat (Lower)	♮ Natural (Normal = no change)	♯ Sharp (Higher)

♯ **Sharp** ↑ = raises a note by 1 step
(raises the finger by 1 step)

♭ **Flat** ↓ = lowers a note by 1 step
(lowers the finger by 1 step)

♮ **Natural** = puts a note back to its original pitch

In order, arrange the accidental from highest to lowest and name the accidentals.

ACCIDENTALS	NAME

The sharp sign should be drawn on the same space or line as the note.

Trace the sharp signs below and draw THREE more through any line and THREE more in any space.

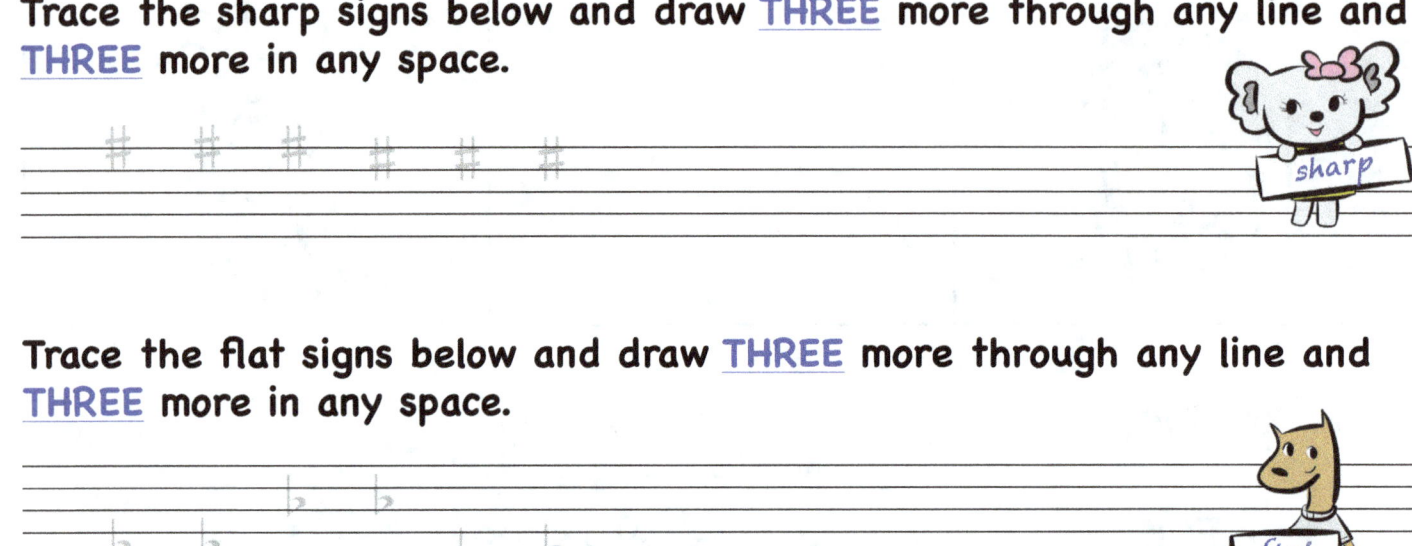

Trace the flat signs below and draw THREE more through any line and THREE more in any space.

Trace the natural signs below and draw THREE more through any line and THREE more in any space.

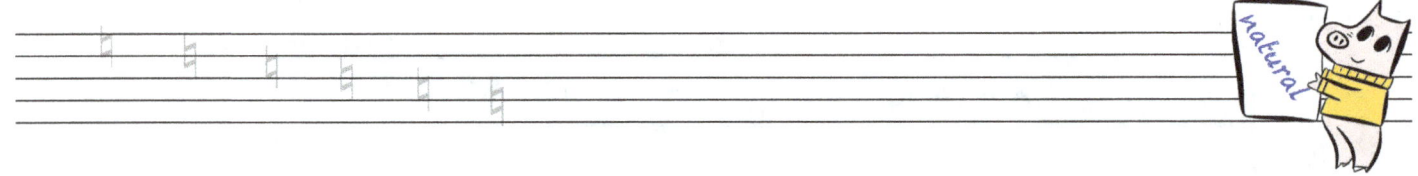

The accidental signs are always drawn before the note. When labeling a note the accidental signs are written after the note.

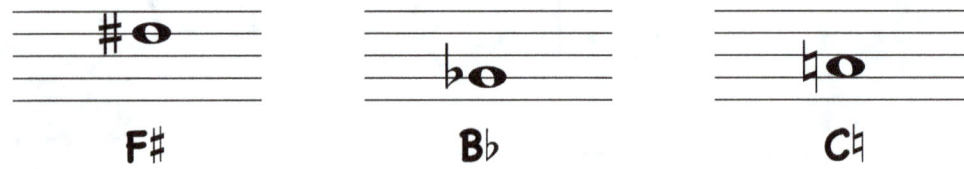

Put a sharp (♯) before every note.

Put a flat (♭) before every note.

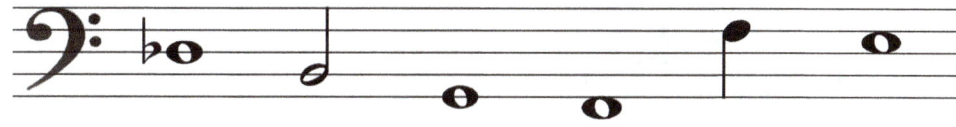

Now name the notes above.

Name the notes below.

G♯

D String

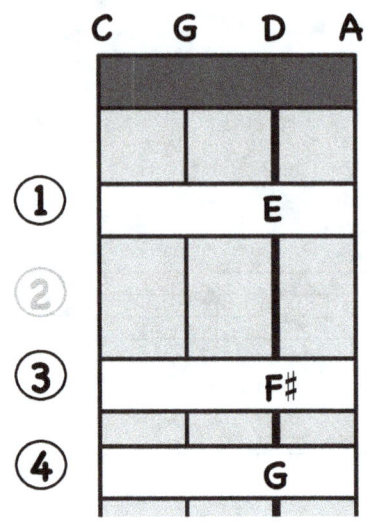

(we are going to skip finger 2)

Copy each note below and their fingering accordingly.

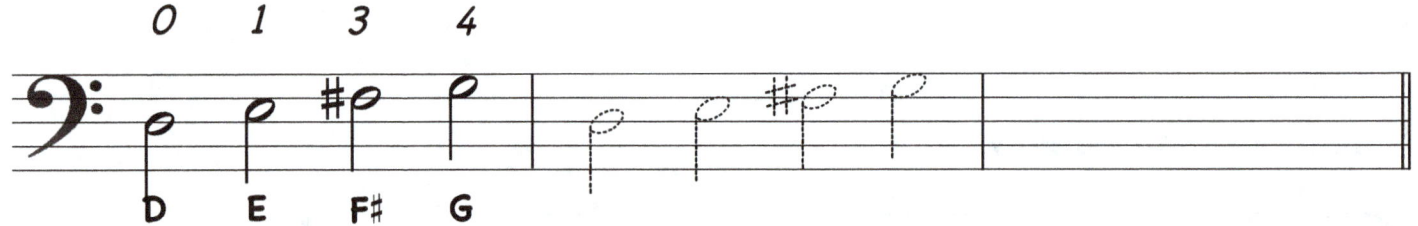

Name the notes and their fingering accordingly.

F#

Two children went to the pet shop. Each tries to touch the animals with their finger. Color the animals according to the finger they used.

RED   GREEN   BLUE

Strings and Note Names

Remember the letters you use in music to name the music notes? What are they? _____

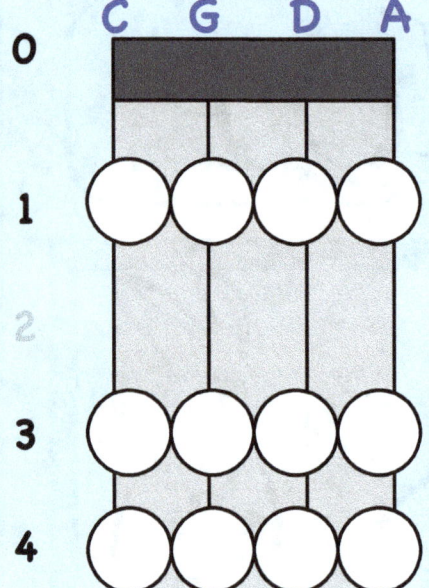

Name each fingering of the main lines on the cello according to your music alphabet.
(Finger 0, 1, 3, 4)

The open strings are already given.

Make sure that there is a SHARP on the 3rd finger on the D and A string.

Which finger tab has no sharps? _____

Pluck each note on your cello while saying the letter names of each note starting on the open C string.

Now try playing and naming each note backwards starting on finger 4 on the A string.

A String

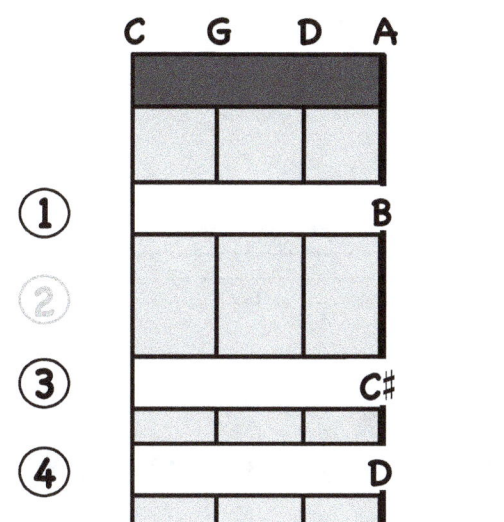
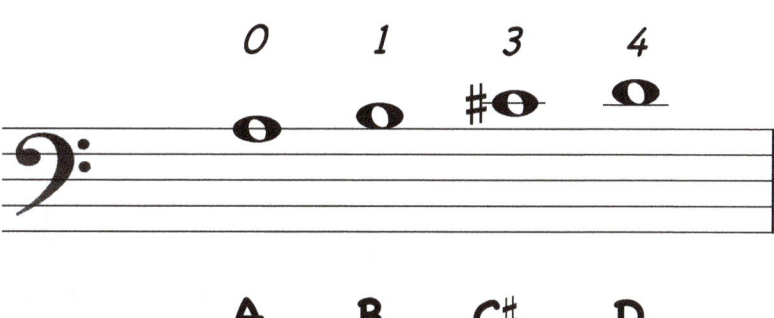

Copy each note below and their fingering accordingly.

Fill in the blanks.

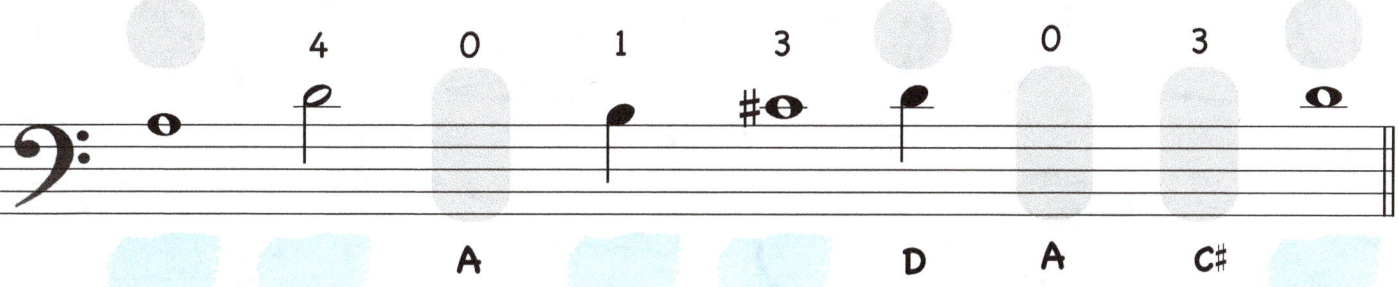

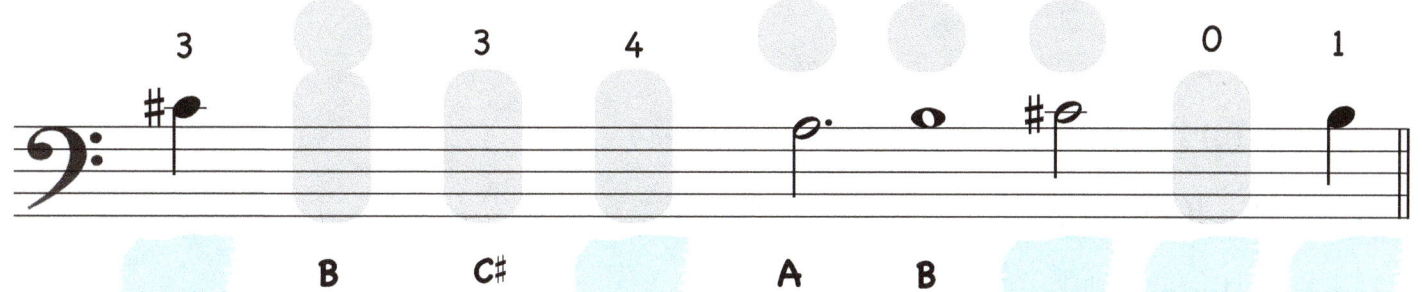

Draw the notes of these fingering on the A string and name the notes.

Tommy and his friends all finish their music lessons at the same time. Who reaches home 1st?

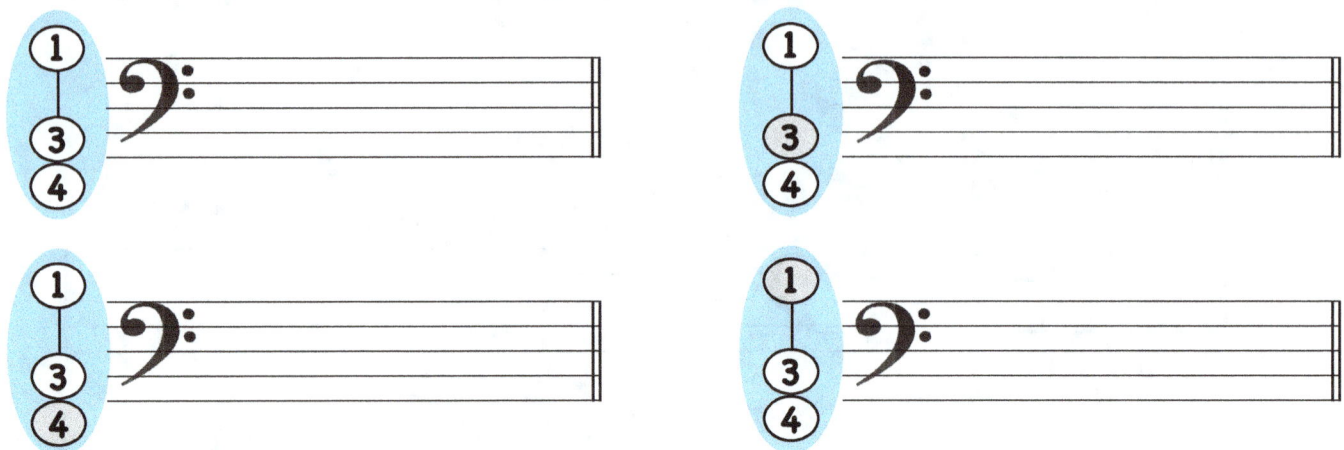

Pete the Pig:

Max the Turtle:

Tommy the Kangaroo:

Kate the Penguin:

Revision D and A Strings

Using whole notes, draw the notes as shown, including the open string notes.

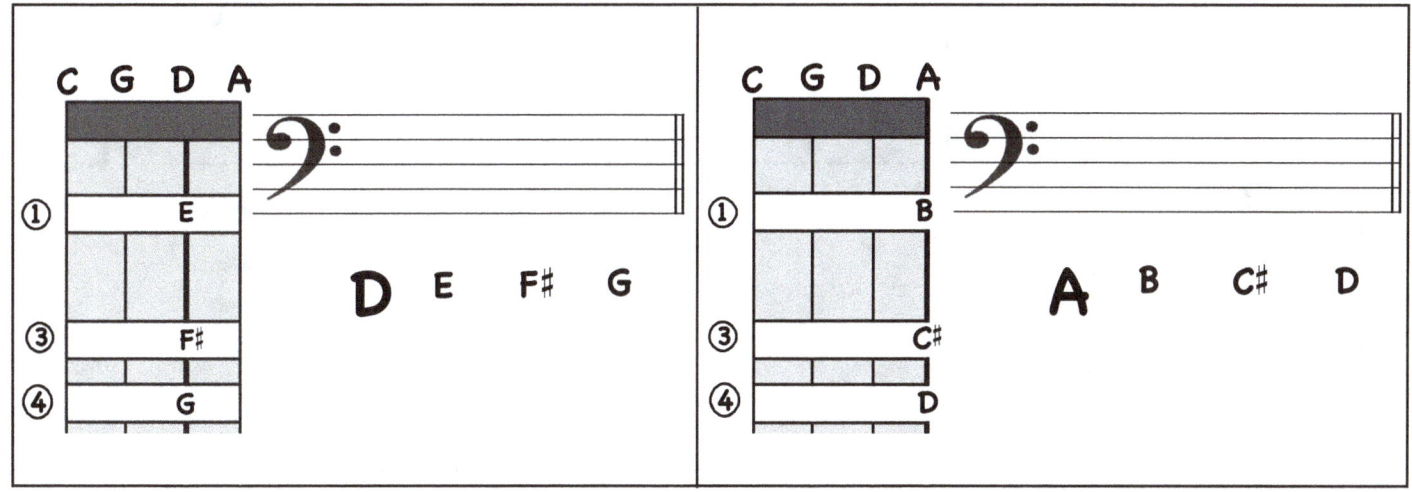

Which fingering do you use on these notes?

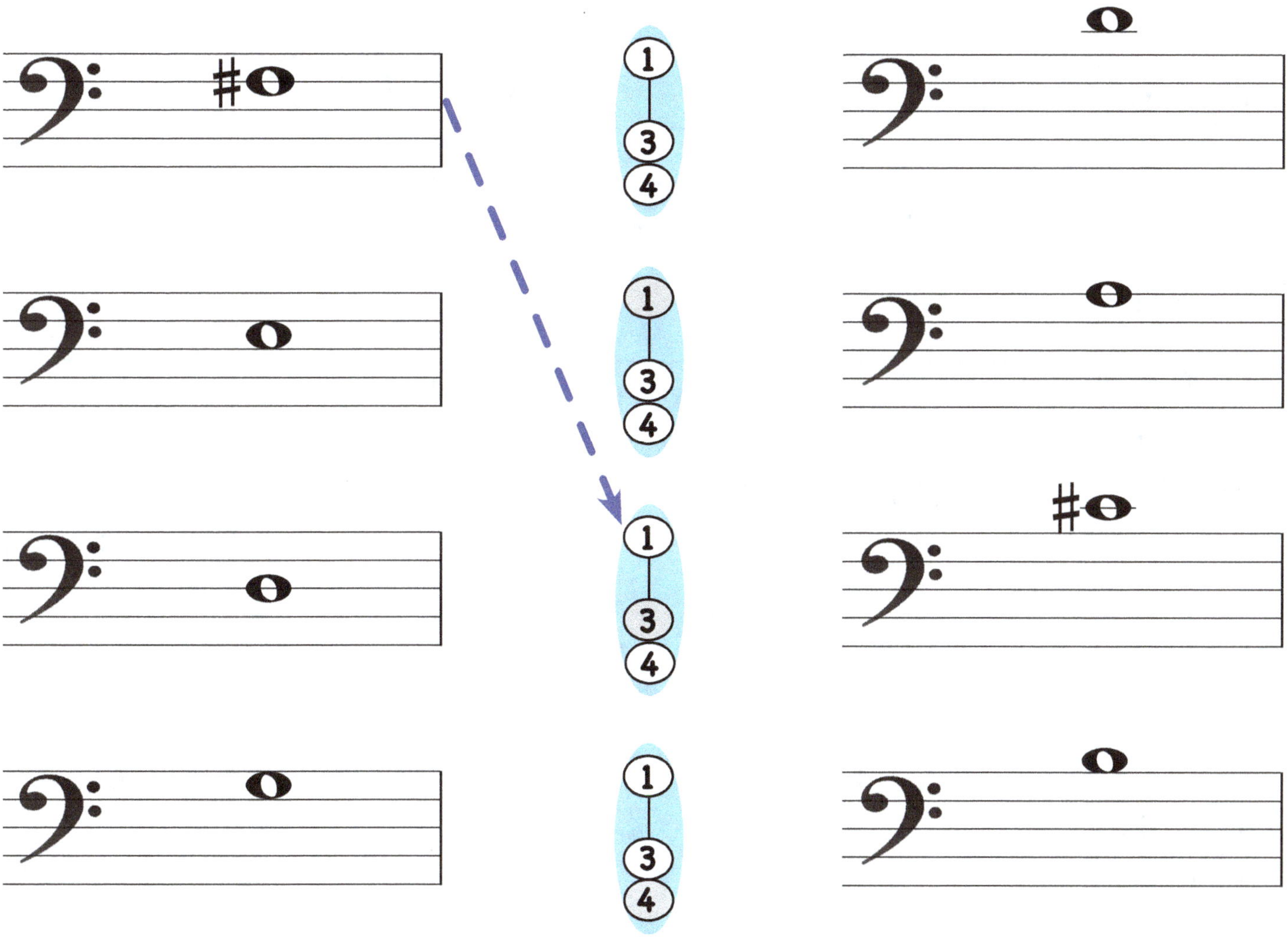

Name each note according to the fingering and label it on the string.

STRINGS	FINGERING	NAME OF THE NOTE
A string	4	D
D string		G
A string	1	
D string	3	
D string		E
A string		A

G String

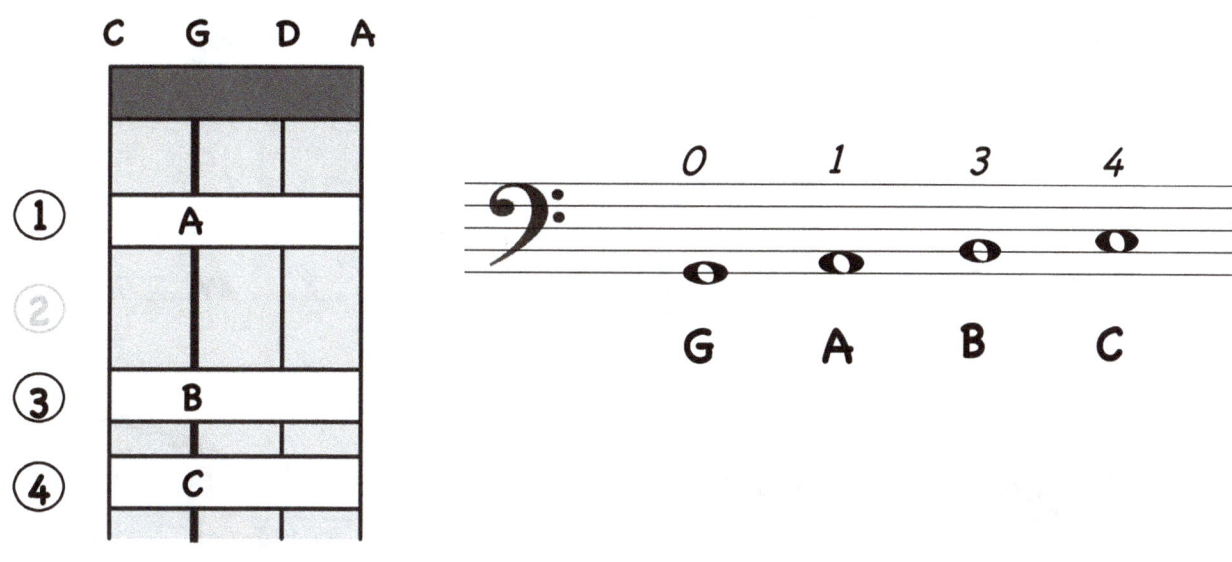

Copy each note below and their fingering.

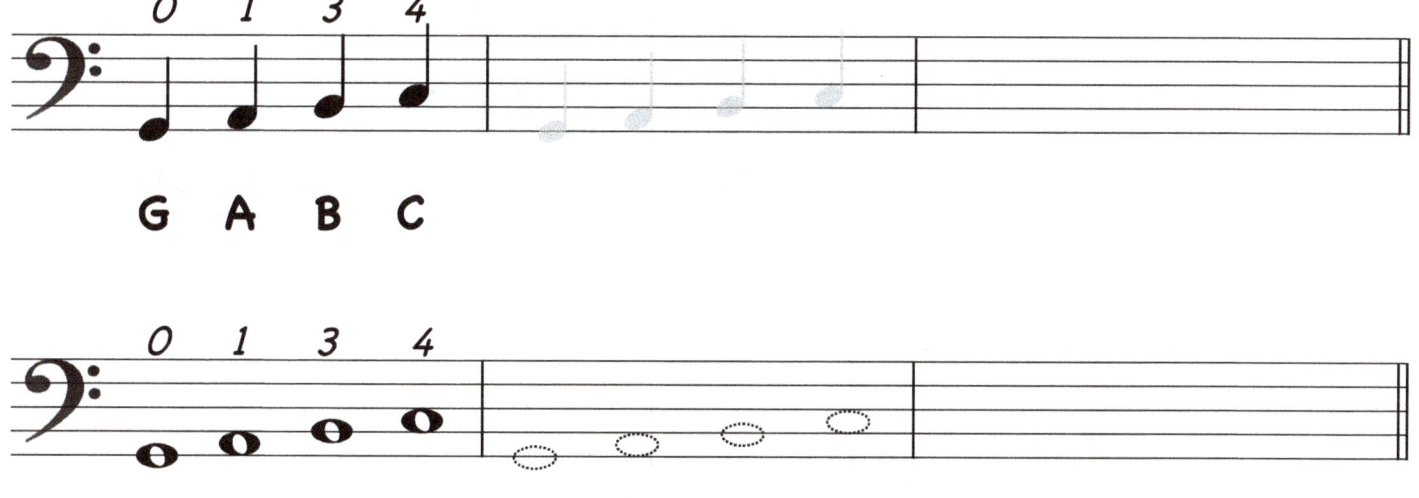

Draw the notes of these fingerings and name the notes on the G string.

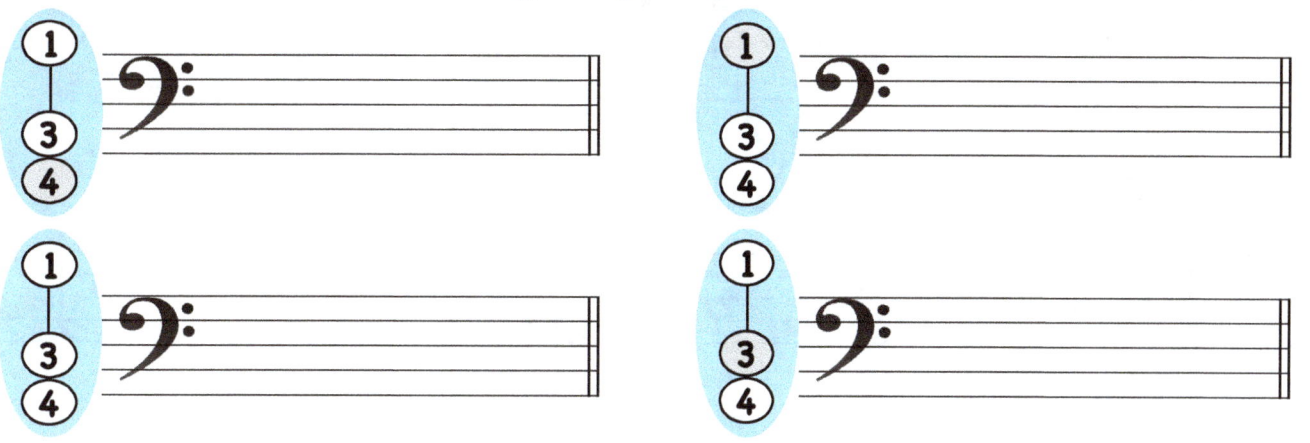

46

Which fingers are used to play these notes?

Color the fingering and name the note.

Name the notes.

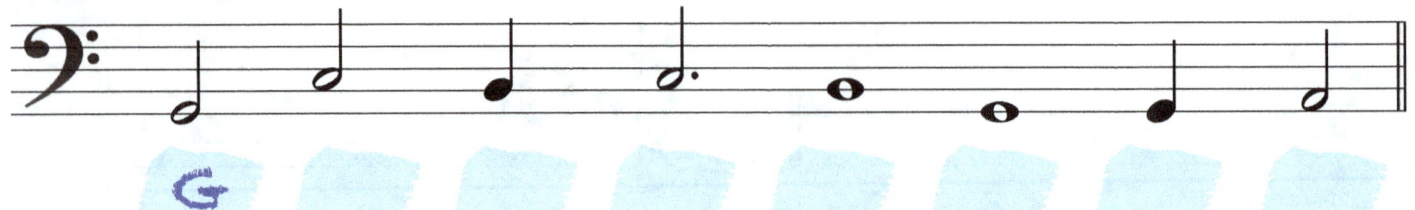

C String

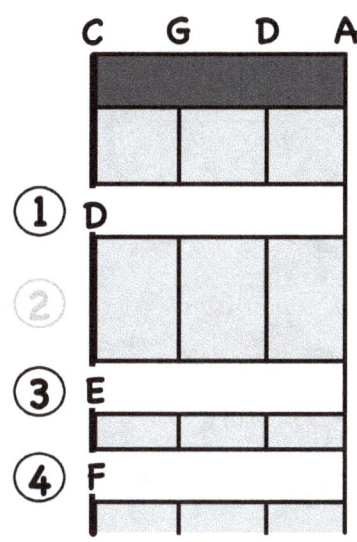
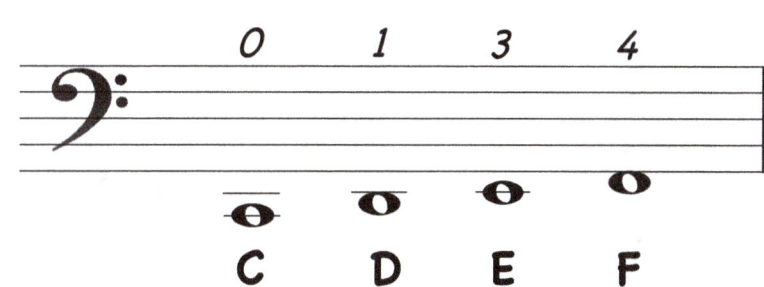

Copy each note below and their fingering.

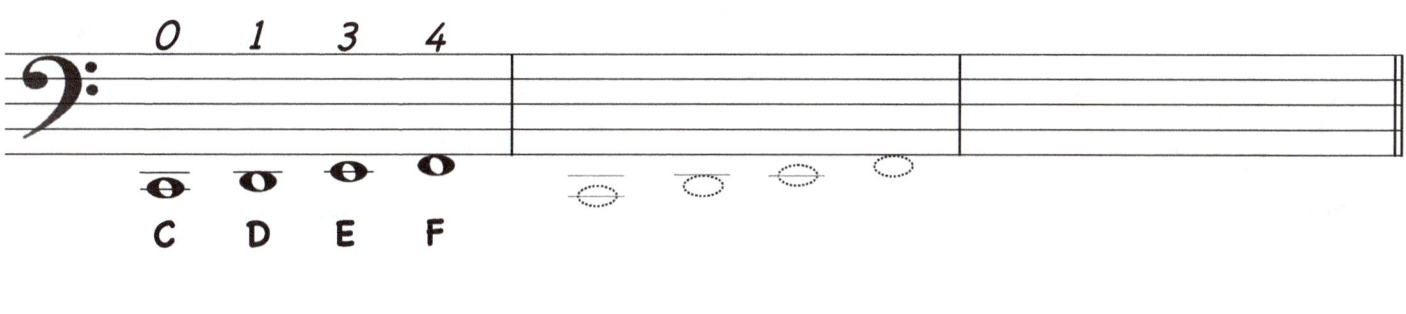

Now play these notes on the cello while naming them aloud.

Name the notes and its fingering.

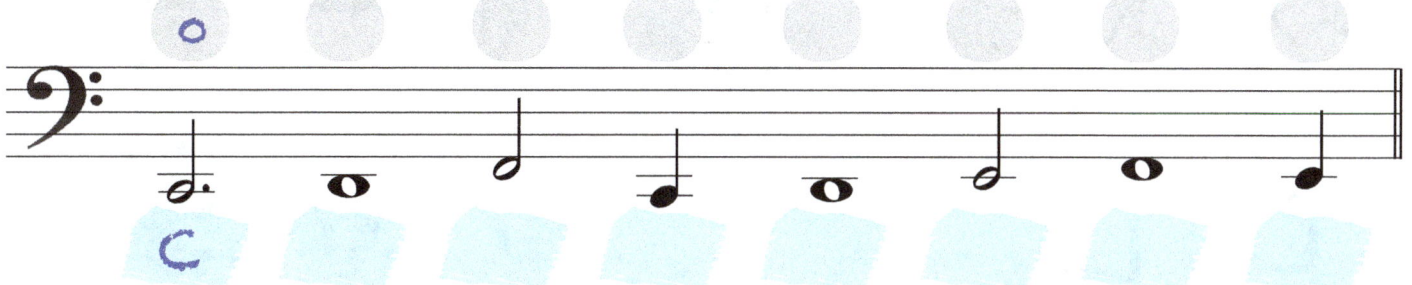

48

Match the fingering on these notes.

Revision (on all strings)

1. Draw all the open string notes according to the name given.

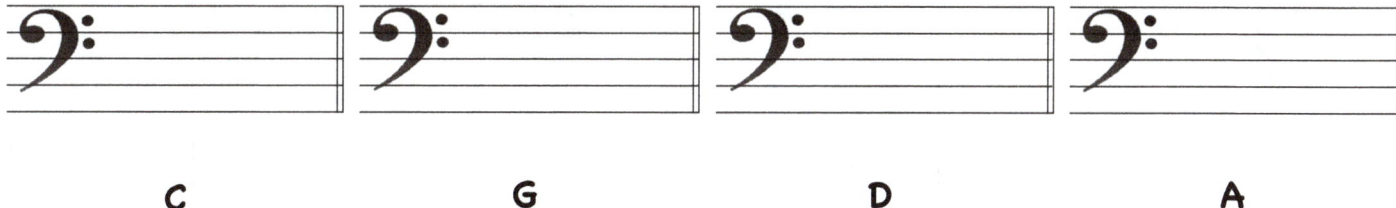

    C   G   D   A

2. Name the string where each of these notes are found.

G	D String		A	
E			D	
C			C	
C#			D	
F			F#	

3. Write down the fingering and name the notes.

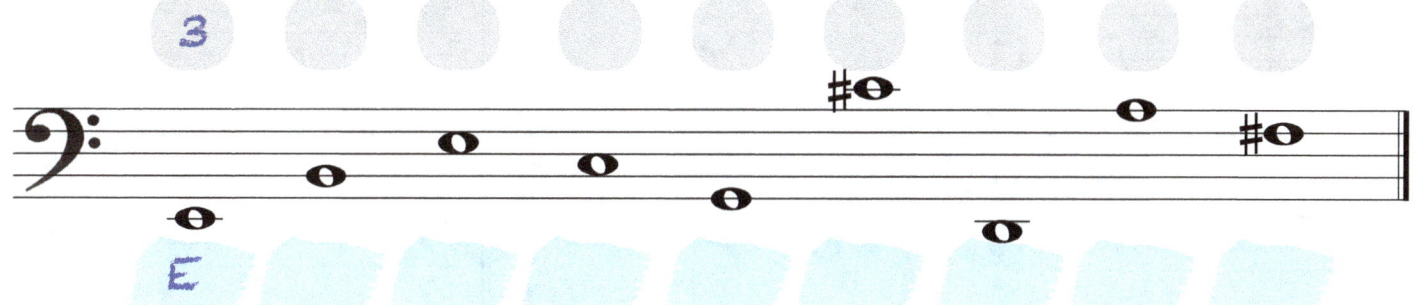

4. Draw these notes on the staff.

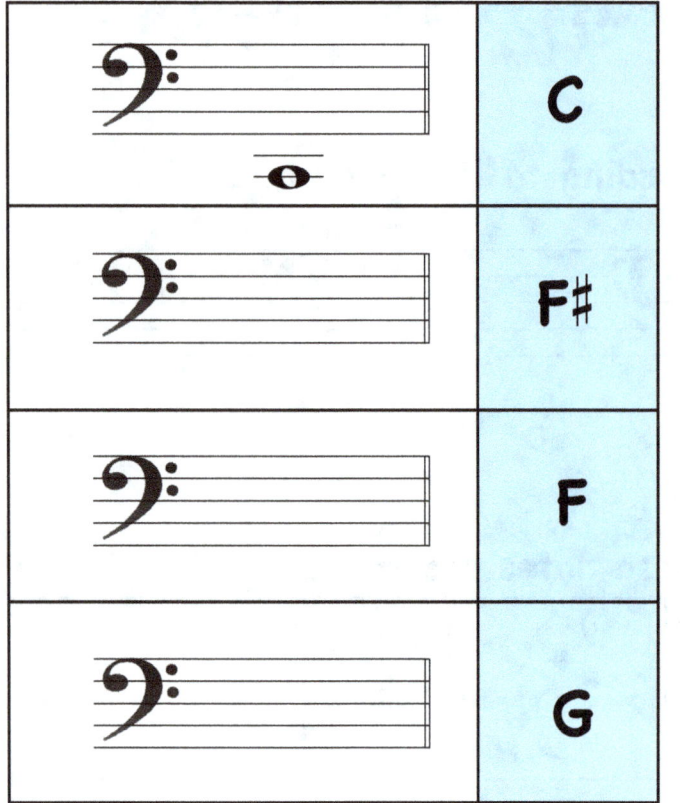

5. Draw 2 different notes and color in their fingering.

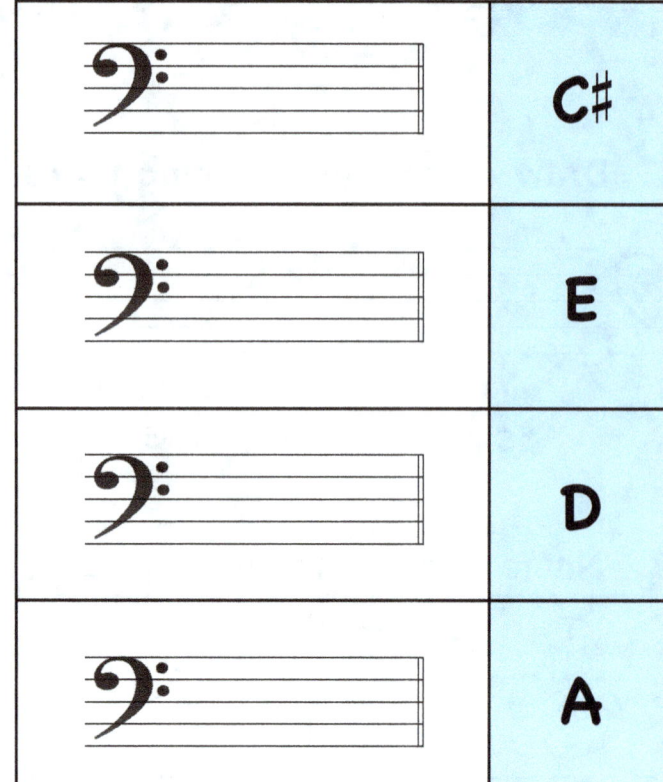

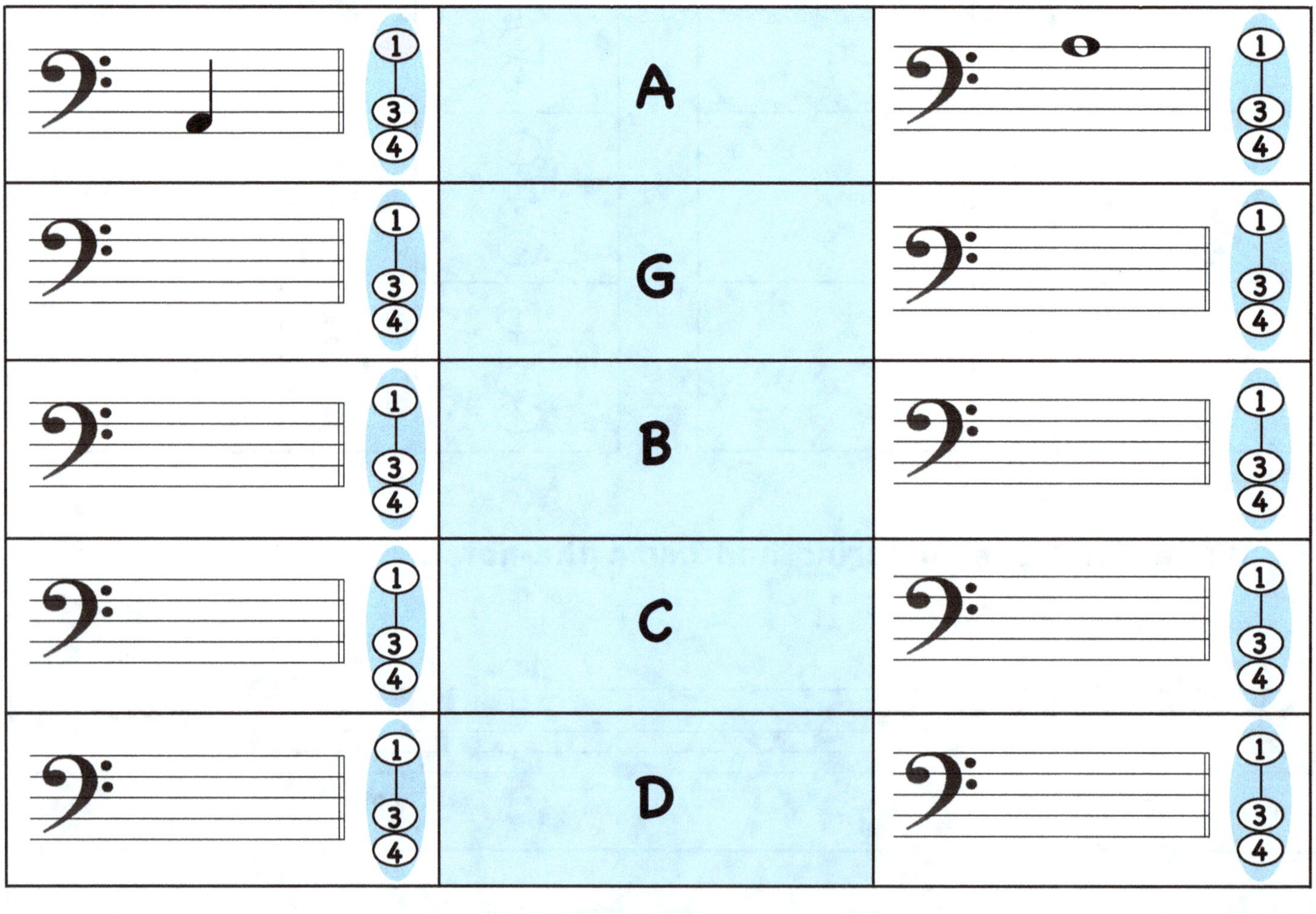

Name: _____   Date: _____

Test

TOTAL MARKS: _____/100

1. Name these notes. _____/12

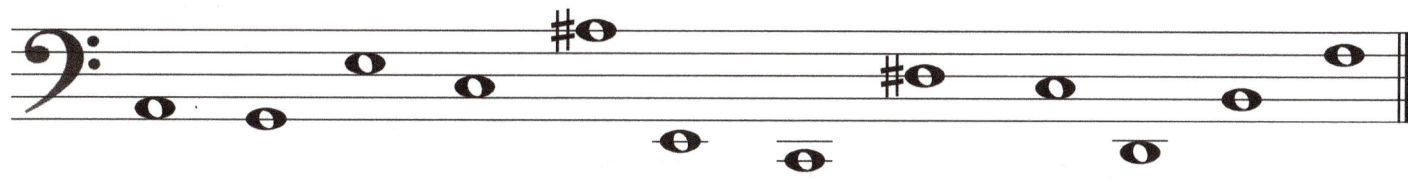

2. Label above each note in question 1 with the correct fingering.
   (0, 1, 3, 4)   _____/12

3. How many beats are these notes? _____/12

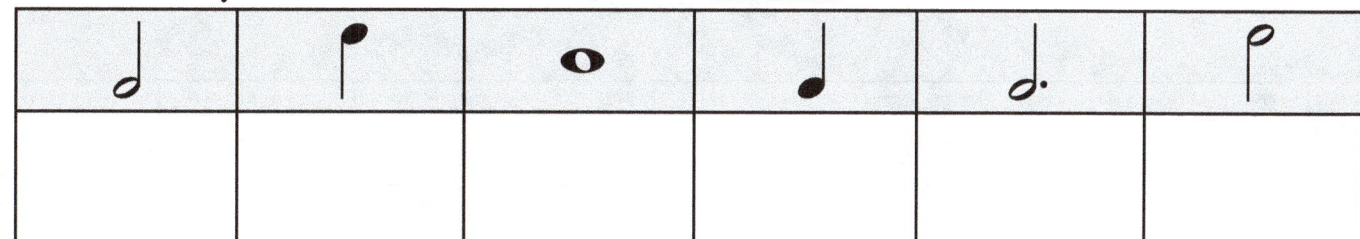

4. How many beats are these rests? _____/12

5. Complete each measure with one missing note. _____/8

6. Complete each measure with one missing rest.   /8

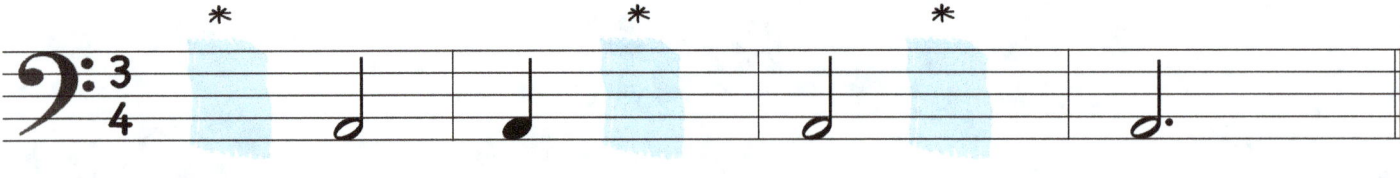

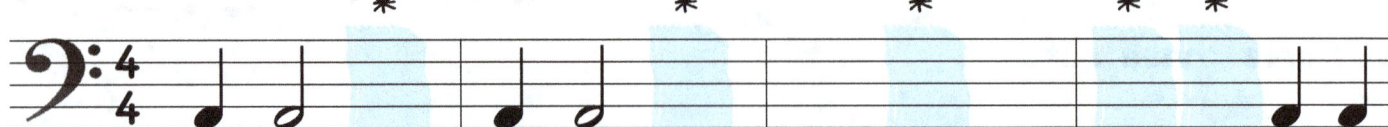

7. Write the beats and the time signature.   2/4 3/4 4/4   /20

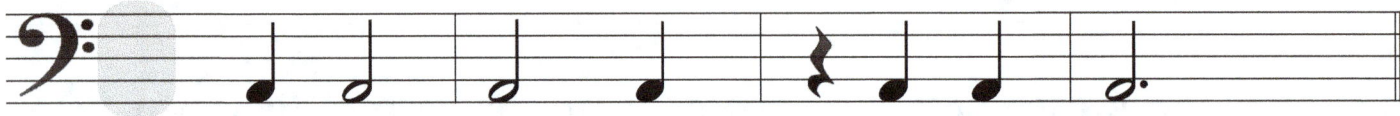

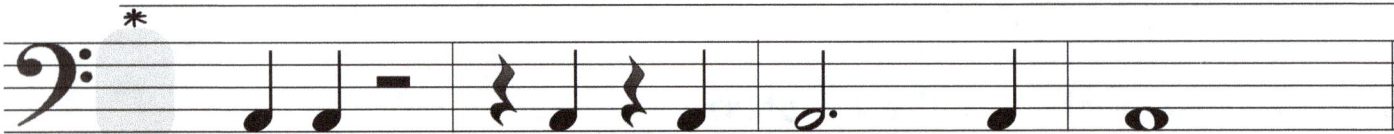

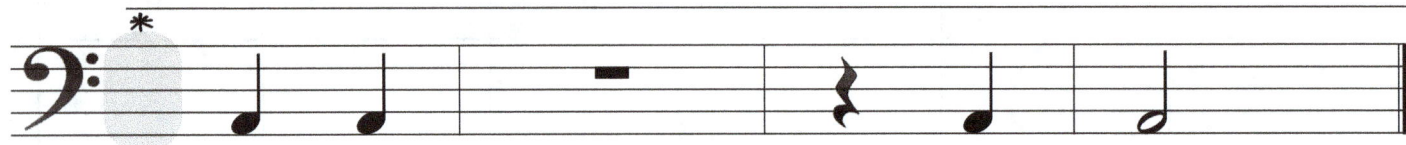

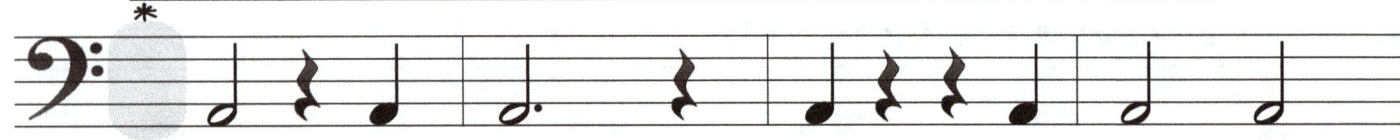

8. Fill in the two different fingerings for these notes and indicate the string they are on.   /16